BARON CROCODILE

The Story
of Horatio Nelson

Elizabeth Newbery

HORATIO NELSON was born in Norfolk in 1758, the son of a country parson. When he was a teenager he had a powerful feeling that one day he would become a great hero.

Nelson aged about 21.

I thought he was a reckless daredevil.

He was quite short, skinny and very vain!

He broke my heart!

He saved Britain!

He was so brave!

Francis (Fanny) Nisbet

Nelson was fearless in battle and overcame serious illness and terrible wounds. He took huge risks to win three great battles for Britain. He was a brilliant commander who inspired his men to fight bravely alongside him. And through Nelson, Britain became the strongest sea power in the world until modern times.

Nelson aged about 43.

Emma Hamilton

Horatia Nelson Thompson

The Arctic Ocean is always frozen. Ships going to the Arctic had to be specially thickened to prevent them being trapped and broken up by the ice.

Thick sea fog makes navigating in the Arctic very risky. In Nelson's day, helmsmen steering the boat relied on the sound of foghorns, drums and ships' bells to avoid crashing into other ships and icebergs. This bell comes from the *San Josef* (see page 8).

This is Nelson's story...

Nelson joined the Royal Navy as a midshipman (trainee officer) aged 12. He found life at sea scary at first, but soon grew to love it. When Nelson was 14, he begged Captain Lutwidge to take him to the Arctic. Boys were not usually allowed to go to such dangerous places.

Ships were loaded up with plenty of food and drink, thick clothes and bricks to build shelters in case the ships got crushed by ice or even rammed by huge whales!

None of this scared the young Nelson. He was a daredevil and once even put his own life in danger. One dark, foggy night he left the ship (which was strictly against the rules) to track down polar bears. As a huge animal reared up out of the mist, Nelson took aim but his musket failed to go off!

This painting shows Nelson about to club the bear with his musket. If the ice hadn't cracked open who do you think would have come off worse?

Just as he was about to club the bear with his musket, a deep crack opened in the ice separating him from the animal.

Then the fog cleared. Captain Lutwidge saw that Nelson was in great danger and immediately ordered his men to fire a cannon to scare the bear off. As the cannon exploded with a loud **BANG**! the bear hesitated and then slunk away. A very lucky escape!

Captain Lutwidge gave me a good telling off. But I wanted a bear skin for my father!

All aboard

A large ship was home to about 850 men. There were officers who gave orders, men who had special skills such as the carpenter, marines (sea-going soldiers who kept order) and seamen who did all the hard work needed to keep the ship afloat. Everyone was under the command of the captain.

Captain of Marines

Who did what?

Captain

Master (in charge of navigation)

Lieutenants (helped to run the ship)

Midshipmen (trainee officers)

Petty Officers

Surgeon

Schoolmaster

Servants (served the officers)

Purser (in charge of supplies)

Carpenters

Cook

Marines

Gunners

Sailmakers

Boatswain (in charge of the sails and rigging)

Caulkers (kept the ship watertight)

Able Seamen

Powder Monkeys (boys who brought gunpowder to the gunners)

Carpenter

Purser

Able Seaman

Cook

Women at sea

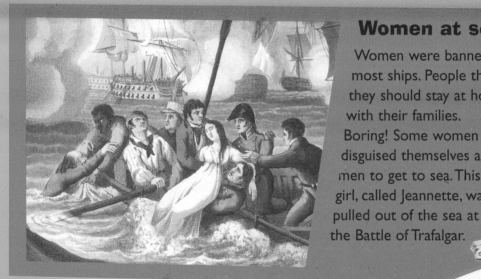

Women were banned from most ships. People thought they should stay at home with their families. Boring! Some women disguised themselves as men to get to sea. This girl, called Jeannette, was pulled out of the sea at the Battle of Trafalgar.

Nelson's rise to the top

Admiral of the Fleet was the highest rank in the Royal Navy. Below admirals were vice-admirals and below them, rear-admirals. All three ranks commanded fleets of ships and directed battles. They were entitled to fly their own flag on their ship (a flagship).

Vice-Admiral of the White -	1804
Vice-Admiral of the Blue -	1801
Rear-Admiral of the Red -	1799
Rear-Admiral of the Blue -	1797
Commodore -	1796
Post-captain -	1779
Commander -	1778
Lieutenant -	1777
Midshipman -	1771

Nelson's Column,
Trafalgar Square, London

Nelson had to spend six years at sea as a midshipman before he could take an exam to become a lieutenant. After that, hard work, important friends and officers helped him to be promoted to post-captain when he was only 21.

The Navy was the life for me. Whenever I was on land, I couldn't wait to get back to sea again!

Nelson learnt to take command of 'prizes' – enemy ships that were captured and sold off. The money was divided amongst the crew – which made some captains and officers very rich! Here he is boarding the *San Josef*.

Midshipman Nelson learnt everything about navigating ships in all weathers and climates. He saw the courage of the seamen who worked aloft in the sails and discovered how flags signalled messages. He mastered complicated instruments and learnt how to command men.

During this time he sailed to India, North America, the West Indies, Central America and Canada. He captured prizes, chased and caught American privateers (pirates allowed by law to attack enemy ships), and was given the command of his first ship.

Seamen found their way at sea using the position of the stars in the sky. This figure of a lieutenant holds an octant for measuring the angle between the horizon and the stars. From that he could plot the position of his ship on a special chart.

Some years later, Nelson was in the West Indies. There he met Frances Nisbet, a young widow who had a son called Josiah. Two years later they married and Nelson, his new wife and stepson returned to England. They lived quietly until 1793 when everything changed. War broke out between Britain and France and the Royal Navy was needed to fight the enemy at sea.

Frances (Fanny) Nisbet was kind and caring.

All hands ahoy!

Life in Nelson's navy was very hard, especially for ordinary seamen. Many captains wouldn't give them shore leave because they might not come back – especially if they had been press-ganged. Many seamen spent years at sea without ever leaving the ship.

Press-gangs

In wartime, more seamen were needed to work the ships so gangs were sent to round up men. They were dragged off and taken on board where they were forced to serve in the navy.

There were more rats than men aboard ships. They made a tasty meal – 'as good as rabbits'. Eeeeeek!

Each man was allowed weekly rations of biscuits, meat, dried peas, oatmeal, sugar, butter and cheese.

Water kept in barrels for a long time became green and slimy. Men drank beer, wine or rum instead.

Do you think these sailors are having a hard time? Or are they enjoying themselves?

Disease

Seamen were crammed together in the lower gun decks where there wasn't even enough room to stand up straight. This meant that killer diseases such as typhus (caused by fleas on rats) spread like wildfire. Disease killed more men than battles at sea. So seamen had to scrub the decks every day to keep the ship clean.

cat-o'-nine tails

Punishment

Seamen were flogged with the cat-o'-nine tails if they disobeyed strict rules. Everybody had to watch, making it extra shameful. When it was over, the man's back was sloshed with sea water to help it heal. Arrrhhh!

Meanwhile in France...

The winter of 1788 was very cold and ordinary people were starving and fed up with having to pay high taxes to the government. At the same time, the French King Louis XVI and Queen Marie Antoinette and other nobles were living in great luxury.

It was so cold in France that people had to use gunpowder to blow vegetables out of the ground!

Eventually, riots broke out and ordinary people executed many nobles. The French Revolution had started! (A revolution is a great struggle to overthrow the government by force and put a new government in its place). Then in 1793, the king and queen were beheaded in front of huge jeering crowds.

The king and queen of France were beheaded with a killing machine called a guillotine.

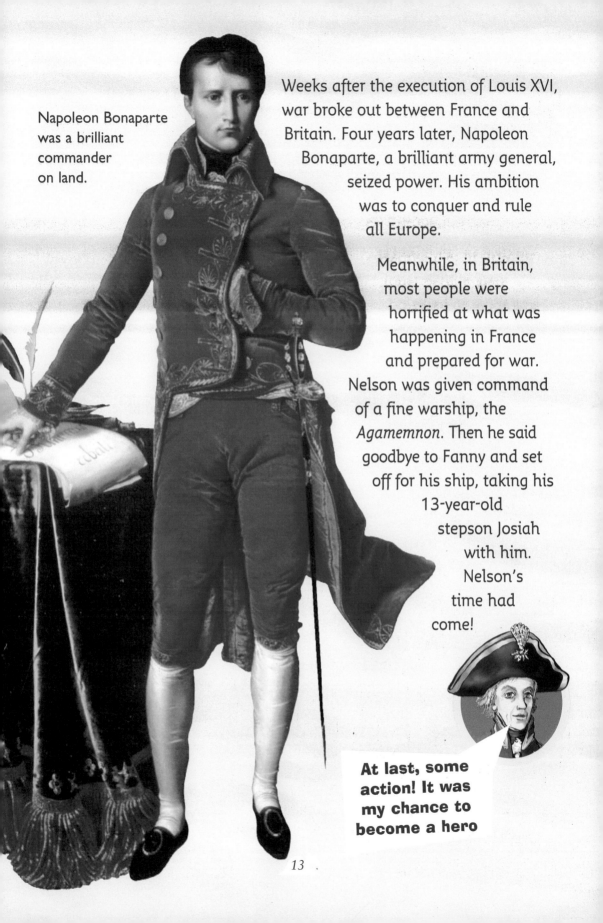

Napoleon Bonaparte was a brilliant commander on land.

Weeks after the execution of Louis XVI, war broke out between France and Britain. Four years later, Napoleon Bonaparte, a brilliant army general, seized power. His ambition was to conquer and rule all Europe.

Meanwhile, in Britain, most people were horrified at what was happening in France and prepared for war. Nelson was given command of a fine warship, the *Agamemnon*. Then he said goodbye to Fanny and set off for his ship, taking his 13-year-old stepson Josiah with him. Nelson's time had come!

At last, some action! It was my chance to become a hero

13

It was while Britain was at war with France that Nelson was badly wounded. In Corsica he was on land when a cannon ball shattered stones in his face blinding him in one eye.

A year later, while under fire at night in Tenerife, Nelson was shot in the right arm. Blood spurted everywhere!

During the Battle of the Nile, Nelson was badly wounded on his forehead. A large flap of skin fell over his good eye and temporarily blinded him. Very scary!

In Nelson's day surgeons were trained to cut off wounded limbs as quickly as possible. Over half the patients died of shock or infection to the wound.

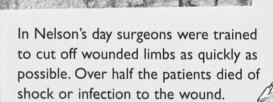

A surgeon's medicine chest.

Nelson knew that if he was going to survive his injury he would have to have his arm amputated. He ordered the ship's surgeon to get his knives and saws ready.

Nelson was taken down to the dimly lit cockpit where the surgeon's mates held him down on the makeshift operating table. Then the surgeon sliced through the flesh and sawed through the bone. Next he sewed flaps of muscle over the end to make a neat stump. Remember there were no anaesthetics or disinfectants, but Nelson didn't cry out once! Afterwards Nelson was given drugs made from poppies (opium) to ease the terrible pain.

I was really fed up because I thought that no-one would want a one-handed admiral

After the fighting was over he returned to England. Fanny nursed him slowly back to health and comforted him when he felt miserable and in pain.

Nelson had to learn to write with his left hand. This is his very first letter.

...y will be able to give me a frigate to convey the remains of my carcase to England, God Bless You my Dear Sir & Believe me your most obliged & faithful

Horatio Nelson

You will excuse my scrawl considering it's my first attempt —

The Battle of the Nile, 1 August 1798

A year later, Nelson had just about recovered from the loss of his arm and was looking forward to going to sea again. Meanwhile, spies reported that Napoleon was assembling warships and thousands of troops in the south of France. What was the enemy up to? Nelson was sent to find out!

When he arrived in the Mediterranean, Napoleon had already left – but where was he going? For the next two months Nelson searched the sea looking for the enemy. One day a lookout spotted the distant masts of the French fleet in Aboukir Bay, near Alexandria, Egypt's main port at the mouth of the River Nile (see map page 30).

Napoleon's admirals were caught off-guard. Most of his men were ashore gathering supplies and the French ships were unprepared for attack. Nelson seized the opportunity!

Imagine how shocked Napoleon's men were when they saw their ships being attacked!

This expensive silver cup was presented to Nelson after the Battle of Nile. Can you see the handles in the shape of Egyptian goddesses?

Up went flags signalling the message 'Enemy in sight!' and drums beat out the message 'Clear for action!' A great battle took place and Nelson succeeded in capturing or destroying most of Napoleon's warships. 218 British sailors were killed and 678 wounded – France lost six times as many with 1700 killed or drowned, 1500 wounded and 3300 taken prisoner. It was seen as a great victory for Britain.

After the Battle of the Nile, I became a big hero. I was promoted too, and made Baron Nelson of the Nile

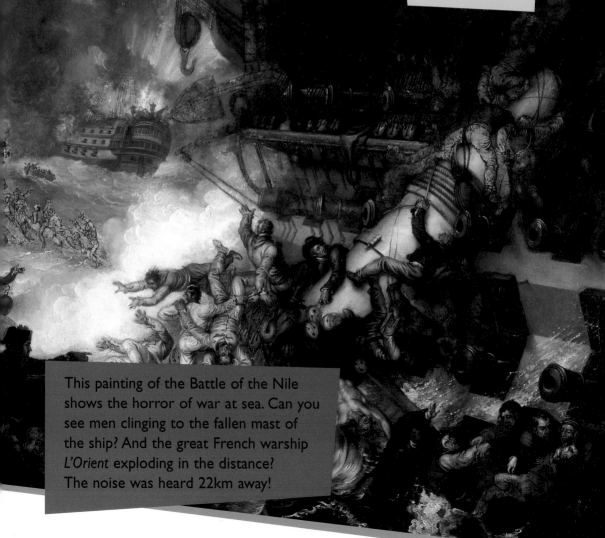

This painting of the Battle of the Nile shows the horror of war at sea. Can you see men clinging to the fallen mast of the ship? And the great French warship *L'Orient* exploding in the distance? The noise was heard 22km away!

Nelson had won a great victory and now he was ready for a break. He decided to go to Italy to repair his ships. There he stayed with Sir William Hamilton, the British Ambassador and his beautiful young wife, Emma. Sir William was much older than Emma. Although he was very fond of his wife, his great love was his priceless collection of ancient Greek vases.

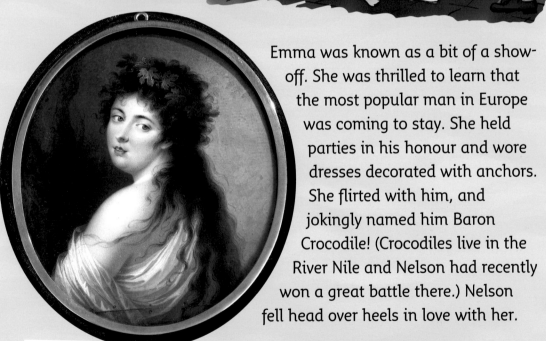

Emma was known as a bit of a show-off. She was thrilled to learn that the most popular man in Europe was coming to stay. She held parties in his honour and wore dresses decorated with anchors. She flirted with him, and jokingly named him Baron Crocodile! (Crocodiles live in the River Nile and Nelson had recently won a great battle there.) Nelson fell head over heels in love with her.

Emma Hamilton wasn't just a pretty face – she was interested in politics too.

Nelson was having such a good time with Emma that he ignored demands to go back to Britain – including those from his faithful wife, Fanny.

I loved Emma so much that I didn't care what people thought of me!

Eventually Nelson decided to return home. He went overland in a carriage accompanied by Sir William and Emma. The three of them lived together near London. Many people were very shocked, especially by Nelson's behaviour towards his wife. Fanny was very, very upset but she did not let it show.

Emma and Nelson had a daughter called Horatia. This is a picture of her. Although they loved her very much they tried to pretend she was the daughter of another sailor. Horatia never knew who her mother and father were.

While Nelson was at sea, Horatia asked him for a dog. He sent her this gold necklace decorated with a dog. Do you think she was disappointed?

Nelson finally arrived back in Britain more than two years after the Battle of the Nile. And what a welcome he got! Thousands of people turned out to see the most famous admiral in the world. He was greeted with magnificent firework displays and celebrations were held in his honour up and down the country. He was given medals from rulers all over Europe including the Tsar of Russia and the Sultan of Turkey.

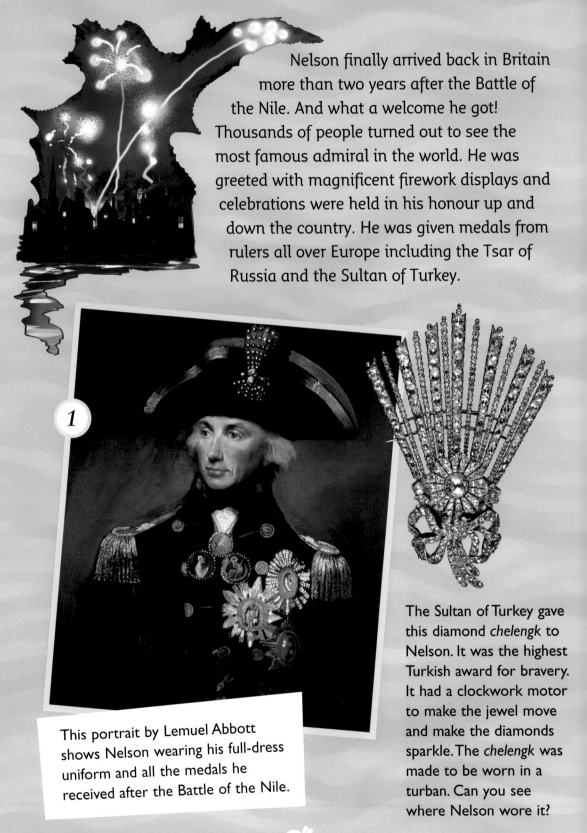

1

This portrait by Lemuel Abbott shows Nelson wearing his full-dress uniform and all the medals he received after the Battle of the Nile.

The Sultan of Turkey gave this diamond *chelengk* to Nelson. It was the highest Turkish award for bravery. It had a clockwork motor to make the jewel move and make the diamonds sparkle. The *chelengk* was made to be worn in a turban. Can you see where Nelson wore it?

Wherever Nelson went he had his portrait painted. He sat for artists in Italy, Austria, Germany and England. Some artists painted him as a great hero but others showed him just as he was – thin and worn-out.

Here are three portraits of Nelson painted after the Battle of the Nile.

This is the life – fame, presents and hundreds of people who welcome me wherever I go

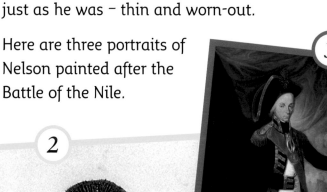

Leonardo Guzzardi painted this portrait of Nelson in Italy. His hat is pushed back to keep it clear of the scar on his forehead.

Look carefully. Which artist do you think painted him as a hero? Which artist saw him as tired and worn-out? And which artist made fun of him? To find out more see page 32.

James Gillray, a cartoonist, drew this picture.

Floating castles

In Nelson's day, the Royal Navy was the largest in the world with nearly a thousand ships – all built of wood and powered by the wind. The biggest warships were like floating castles stuffed with cannon, gunpowder and shot.

Main mast

Platform for seamen working in the riggings and sails

Mizzen mast

Seamen adjusted the sails to make best use of the wind

Foremast

The captain controlled the ship from the quarterdeck

Ratlines were used as ladders for seamen going aloft

Guns could fire one shot a minute

Officers had private cabins at the stern

Seamen shared their living quarters with guns

Going for guns

Ships were 'rated' according to the number of guns they carried.

- First-rates had three decks and 100 guns or more
- Second-rates had three decks and 90 guns or more
- Third-rates had two decks and 64-80 guns.

First-rates, second-rates and third-rates were the warships that won Nelson's great battles. But smaller ships played a big part in battles too, chasing fast enemy ships, patrolling the seas and carrying messages home.

Frigates were some of the most useful ships in a fleet. They were big enough to carry lots of guns but fast enough to be able to escape the enemy.

Firing a cannon

Ammunition is rammed into the cannon

The fuse is lit

Fire!

BANG

The cannon is cooled and cleaned

HMS Victory was a first-rate that carried 104 guns at the Battle of Trafalgar. 6000 oak trees were cut down to build it!

Wooden ships were very difficult to sink. Battles were usually declared over when a crew boarded a ship and overcame the enemy with hand-to-hand fighting using swords, muskets and pistols.

The Battle of Trafalgar, 21 October 1805

After two years of peace, spies reported that Napoleon was planning to invade England. To put an end to his big ideas, Britain had to fight and win a great battle. Nelson was the man chosen to do it.

Saying a loving goodbye to Emma, Nelson raced down to Portsmouth where his ship the *Victory* was waiting. His crew, volunteers and men recruited by the press-gang, included Italian, Indian, Norwegian, Portuguese, Swiss, Dutch, American and French seamen. Everyone cheered Nelson as he climbed aboard. They were going to war with the greatest sailor in the world! He made them feel brave and confident. Of course they would win!

That day, Nelson hoisted his flag on the *Victory* and sailed south to Cadiz (see map page 30) where the French navy was anchored. The British fleet was prepared for battle. Loose equipment was lashed down, the decks were cleared, the guns were run out and the cockpit made ready for the wounded. Gunners stripped to the waist and covered their ears with handkerchiefs to deaden the noise of the guns.

(see map page 30)

Can you see...

- Holes in the sails made by cannon fire?
- Rows of cannon?
- Sailors being rescued?
- Flags which signal the word 'duty'?

Nelson explained his battle plans to his officers.

24

I believed I was the best, that my crew were the best, so we were the best!

Nelson asked his lieutenant to signal a message of encouragement to the rest of the fleet:

'England expects that every man will do his duty'.

Nelson wore this uniform so that his men could recognise him easily in the confusion of the battle.

One of Britain's greatest sea battles was about to begin!

As flags ran up the signal *'Engage the enemy more closely'*, Nelson's ships bore down on them. The French and Spanish (who had sided with the French) opened fire. Within minutes the mizzen mast was down, the wheel had been shot away and for the rest of the battle the *Victory* had to be steered with the tiller!

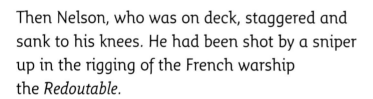

I wasn't afraid to die – I had done my best. My last wish was that people would take care of Emma and Horatia

Then Nelson, who was on deck, staggered and sank to his knees. He had been shot by a sniper up in the rigging of the French warship the *Redoutable*.

Nelson's great friend Captain Hardy ran forward and covered Nelson's face so that the crew wouldn't see that he was badly wounded and lose heart. He was gently carried below to the cockpit where Dr William Beatty, the ship's surgeon attended him. The bullet had pierced Nelson's shoulder and broken his spine.
Dr Beatty and Nelson both knew he was fatally wounded. Look back to page 25 to see the bullet hole in Nelson's uniform.

As he lay dying in agony, Nelson managed to ask how the battle was going. He died shortly after he had heard that it had been won saying, 'Thank God I have done my duty.'

When men died at sea their bodies were usually sewn into their hammocks and dropped over the side of the ship. But Nelson's body was placed in a barrel filled with brandy to preserve it so that he could be buried in London.

When he was dying Nelson asked that his hair should be cut off and given to Emma. And this is it!

This painting shows the death of Nelson. Can you see Reverend Scott, the chaplain, who rubs Nelson's chest to relieve the pain and Dr Beatty who feels Nelson's pulse?

This figurehead was used on the funeral carriage. It represents fame and victory. Can you see it in the picture below?

Weeks later, when a fast ship bought back news to Britain of the great victory, people went wild with excitement. Napoleon's plans had been wrecked! Britain was safe! Britain was the greatest sea power in the world! But when they heard that Nelson was dead the whole country wept.

Huge crowds turned out to watch as Nelson's coffin was carried by barge up the River Thames from Greenwich and then by carriage to St Paul's Cathedral. There his coffin was placed in the crypt under the dome, a place of great honour.

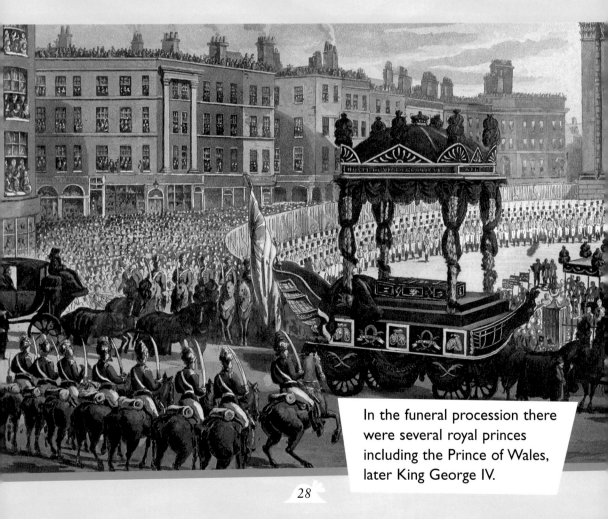

In the funeral procession there were several royal princes including the Prince of Wales, later King George IV.

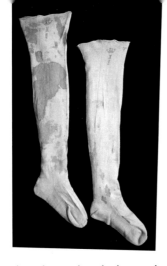

Anything that belonged to Nelson was preserved. These are his stockings stained with the blood of other men who died with Nelson.

People wanted reminders of their hero and all sorts of souvenirs were made, from jugs to jewellery. Poems were written, music composed and plays about the Battle of Trafalgar were staged. Famous artists painted pictures of his great victory and pubs, streets and squares, children and even flowers were named after him. Money was raised to put up memorials to him all over the country including Nelson's Column in Trafalgar Square in London.

The Royal Navy still marks Trafalgar Day, 21 October, with special ceremonies. And people still visit his tomb everyday. Who's your hero?

This brooch contains a piece of Nelson's hair. It was made as a souvenir for one of his close friends.

After Nelson's great victories, fashionable girls wore clothes styled to remind people of the battles.

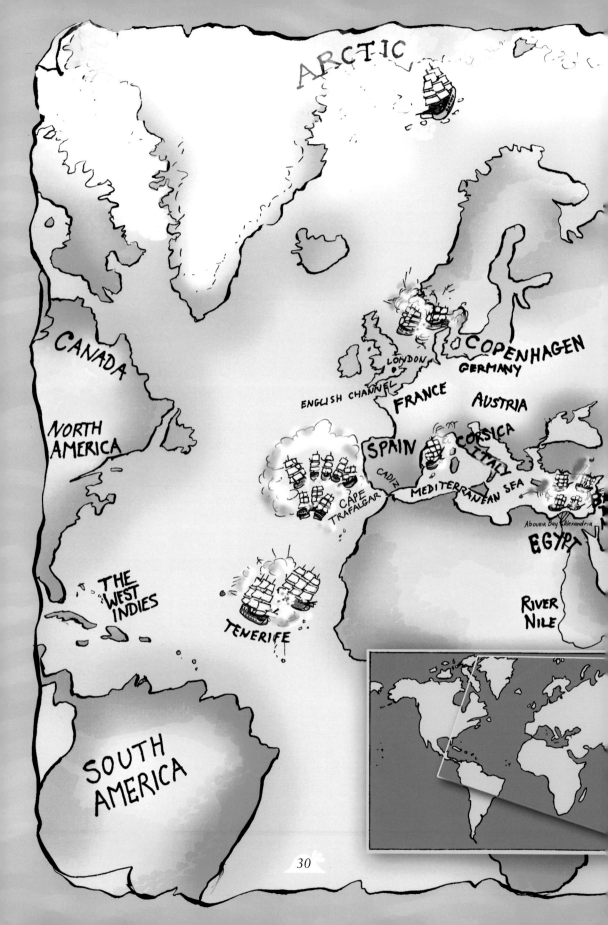

INDIA

Timeline

1758 — Nelson is born

1760 — George III becomes king

1769 — Napoleon Bonaparte is born

1771 — Nelson joins the Royal Navy
as midshipman

1773 — Nelson goes to the Arctic

1777 — Nelson passes exam and becomes
a lieutenant

1787 — Nelson marries Frances Nisbet

1789 — The French Revolution begins

1794 — Nelson is blinded in one eye
while fighting in Corsica

1797 — Nelson loses an arm while fighting
in Tenerife

1798 — The Battle of the Nile

1800 — Nelson returns to Britain with
Sir William and Lady Hamilton

1801 — Horatia is born
The Battle of Copenhagen

1803 — Sir William Hamilton dies

1805 — Nelson is killed at the Battle
of Trafalgar

1806 — Nelson is buried in St Paul's
Cathedral, London

Whatever happened to...

... Emma Hamilton?

Sadly, people ignored Emma after Nelson died. She wasn't even allowed to attend the funeral and died in France in 1815, poor, lonely and forgotten.

... Fanny Nisbet?

Fanny continued to love Nelson faithfully until she died in 1831.

... Josiah Nisbet?

Josiah was not a very good naval officer. He left the navy and became a businessman in France.

... Horatia Nelson?

After her mother died, Horatia, aged 14, went to live with first one family and then another. Both of them were very kind to her. She married a vicar and had nine children. She died in 1881.

Did you know?

① The portrait on page 20 shows Nelson as a great hero. The artist painted the portrait from a sketch. He didn't know that Nelson couldn't wear his hat over his scar and he had to guess what the *chelengk* looked like because he had never seen it.

② This cartoon makes fun of all the gifts and medals Nelson received after the Battle of the Nile. Look how big the artist has made the *chelengk*!

③ The portrait shows Nelson as old and grey. He was only 41 when this picture was painted.

P3 *Rear-Admiral Sir Horatio Nelson* after John Hoppner (*c.*1823-4)

P5 *Nelson and the Bear* by Richard Westall (*c.*1806)

P8 *Nelson boarding a captured ship, 1777,* by Richard Westall (1806)

P9 Fanny Nisbet (Nelson) by Daniel Orme

P14 *Nelson wounded at the Nile* by Guy Head (*c.*1800)

P15 *The Battle of the Nile* by Mather Brown (1825)

P18 *Emma Hamilton* by John Dunn

P19 *Horatia Nelson* after Henry Bone (*c.*1806)

P20 *Rear-Admiral Sir Horatio Nelson* by Lemuel Abbott (1800)

P21 *The Hero of the Nile* by James Gillray (left) *Rear-Admiral Nelson* by Leonardo Guzzardi (right) (1798-9)

P22 *Nelson boarding the San Josef* by George Jones

P25 *The Battle of Trafalgar* by J.M.W. Turner (1822-4)

P27 *The Death of Nelson* by Arthur Devis (1807)

P32 *Emma Hamilton* by George Romney

Acknowledgements

First published in 2005 by the National Maritime Museum, London SE10 9NF

ISBN 0948065672

© National Maritime Museum

1 2 3 4 5 6 7 8 9

A CIP catalogue record for this book is available from the British Library.

Text: Elizabeth Newbery
Editor: Eleanor Dryden
Design: Rachel Hamdi/Holly Mann
Cover design and illustration: Mike Spoor
Print and bind: Colourstream

This book has been published to accompany the exhibition *Nelson & Napoléon* held at the National Maritime Museum, Greenwich.